MUSING

℄

MINGLING VOICES
Series editor: Manijeh Mannani

Give us wholeness, for we are broken.
But who are we asking, and why do we ask?
— PHYLLIS WEBB

National in scope, Mingling Voices draws on the work of both new and established poets, novelists, and writers of short stories. The series especially, but not exclusively, aims to promote authors who challenge traditions and cultural stereotypes. It is designed to reach a wide variety of readers, both generalists and specialists. Mingling Voices is also open to literary works that delineate the immigrant experience in Canada.

Series Titles

sonnets by Jonathan Locke Hart

musing

WITH AN INTRODUCTION BY GORDON TESKEY

AU PRESS

© 2011 Jonathan Locke Hart
Published by AU Press, Athabasca University
1200, 10011 – 109 Street Edmonton, AB T5J 3S8

ISBN 978-1-897425-90-9 (print)
978-1-897425-91-6 (pdf)
978-1-926836-3-86 (epub)

A volume in the Mingling Voices series:
ISSN 1917-9405 (print) 1917-9413 (electronic)

Cover and book design by Natalie Olsen, Kisscut Design.
Cover image by Deborah Elder, *Dream Garden* (1995).
Author photo by Manijeh Mannani.
Printed and bound in Canada by Marquis Book Printing.

Library and Archives Canada Cataloguing in Publication
Hart, Jonathan Locke, 1956–
Musing / Jonathan Locke Hart.

(Mingling voices, ISSN 1917-9405)
Poems.
Also issued in electronic format.
ISBN 978-1-897425-90-9

I. Title. II. Series: Mingling voices

PS8565.A6656M88 2011   C811'.6   C2011-900872-6

We acknowledge the financial support of the Government of
Canada through the Canada Book Fund (CBF) for our publish-
ing activities. ▮✦▮ Canadian   Patrimoine
              Heritage   canadien

For George and Mary

Introduction

℘ Jonathan Locke Hart's five books of poetry cover writing that extends thirty years, although most of his poems appear to have been written between the early 1990s and the mid-2000s. For their sensitivity to nuances of feeling and their technical care, Hart's poems resemble those of another master from Alberta, E.D. Blodgett, to whom one of Hart's books, *Dream China* (2002), is dedicated. But Hart's poems are altogether less intimate than Blodgett's. There is little of Hart's personal life in them, or of our personal lives, in which we are held to one another by the spiderweb of nearly invisible but exceptionally powerful bonds. Nor is Hart a poet like Simon Armitage, for example, whose imagination is rooted deeply in one place, as in almost all

English poets, however much they travel. Although they are always going down lost lanes of Queen Anne's lace, English poets are never lost themselves. They know where they are and where they come from.

Hart is different, and in this, I think, intensely Canadian, or even Australian, for Australians are just like Canadians, only more so. Hart has traveled widely, in China and in every major country in Europe. He has lived long periods in China, but also in England, often at its great universities in Oxford, Cambridge, and London. He has also had extended stays in the United States, at Princeton and especially at Harvard, a university with which he has had close personal connections. Trained in history and English literature, a scholar of the European Renaissance and of Shakespeare, and of the history of colonialism, Hart is a creature of the elite university world — his PhD is from Toronto, where he lived in Massey College — but he is also a citizen of the world outside the universities. His poetry is intensely a poetry of place, place known and felt in historical depth; but the places in question are many. His is not a poetry of roots but of mobility.

One of Hart's heroes and teachers, Marshall McLuhan, spoke not unfavorably of the rootlessness of modern man in the age of modern communications. Another of Hart's heroes and teachers, Northrop Frye, influenced by McLuhan's mentor, Harold Adams Innis, spoke of how Canada, because it is a vast, sparsely populated territory and obsessed, as a result, with communications, is a post-national country just because of this fact. Communications — a transcontinental railway and telegraph, a trans-Canada highway, a growing trade in Canadian books, aircraft, immigration, radio, telecommunications, the Internet — were needed to unite the vast country. But this unifying effort overshot its aim because there was no reason, nor is there now, for communications to stop at national boundaries. Communications, the "extensions of man," as McLuhan called them, break through all boundaries whatever and connect us with the world, and with others in the world, sometimes unpleasantly. Paradoxically, in trying to unite and define itself as a country by means of communications, Canada succeeded in doing the opposite. It became a post-national country.

Every young Canadian (and not only young

Canadians) gets on an airplane as soon as she or he can and flees the country for some other place, for any other place, and preferably for many other places. They do so not out of any particular dislike of Canada (on the contrary) but out of the sense that this is what Canadians do: travel to other places on the globe and experience other cultures as directly as they can. Canadians have a strong sense of home, but this sense of home is, so to speak, dialectically determined by the experience of being away, even by the need to be away. If a Canadian who has lived in the United States for twenty-eight years may venture to say so, this need to be away from home in order to be home is one thing — not the only thing, of course, but an important one — that makes Canadians different from Americans. Americans feel American enough when at home. They feel American enough when abroad, no more, no less. The world is on TV.

Jonathan Hart's poems are widely traveled works. Yet it is not so much a sense of home that they awaken dialectically as it is the sense of consciousness itself, consciousness reflecting on history, on the passage of time and on the specificity of earlier times, the *haecceitas* of the past.

In *Breath and Dust*, the earliest collection of poems, written from the mid-1970s to the late 1990s, Hart starts out in one poem in Canada, with a Canadian title, "Cabin Fever," describing a sparrow that collided with the window and froze there, the river beyond "stacked and heaving / With broken ice." It is a place where "even the dead are cold." But the poem ends with an escape that is provided by books, another mode of communication, books from afar, with their "imported signs," fire and roses (from T.S. Eliot's *Four Quartets*) and the final, sweet, beautifully paced lines, "would that I were young / Again and in your arms." Natural in their longing as they sound, those lines are a canny translation from another place and another time, from a famous, fourteenth-century English lyric poem. Their place at the end of this poem, apart from the emotional relief they provide, has the effect of relieving the Canadian's cabin fever, confined within national boundaries, and opening the way to England. But not today's England. This is the England of another time.

What's naïve about Canadian wanderlust is the supposition that there is a world, a truly other world, that exists elsewhere and now. But in truth the entire planet is becoming much the same, as older, more traditional cultures huddle in pockets and modern communications envelop everything. To get elsewhere you have to go into the past. That is where Hart's historical training comes in and serves him so well as a poet. He knows that to get to a place where we are far enough from home to know home again, we have to turn to the past.

The past is known in books, and Hart is a subtly but deeply learned poet, a *doctus poeta*. In "The Charles" (also from *Breath and Dust*), as he and a friend walk alongside the basketball courts beside the Charles River in Cambridge, Massachusetts, near Harvard, listening to the squeaking shoes, the friend comments, "the only thing real . . . is the jazz of basketball" and "the slow movement of a woman on a bicycle, asserting nothing." The friend is gently reproached for this overly phenomenological view as the poem turns decisively on the word "but," returning us to "books / About books" and "the self-congratulation of critical discourse, finding / Ourselves in smoke." Notwithstanding that "self-congratulation," the point is not as negative as it sounds. Hart is not saying that in reading of the past we fail to find ourselves but are instead lost in smoke. He is saying that only in the smoke of the past, which seems so unreal — for much of what we know of the past has literally gone up in smoke, and books themselves, even in libraries, are very slowly on fire — do we find "the only thing real."

We should not be deceived by the superficially easier, imagist delights of *Dream China* (2002) and *Dream Salvage* (2003) into thinking that these books escape history into pure meditation on the image. Far from it. They meditate on Greek mythology and Roman history, especially the great Roman historian Tacitus, on war in China and in the West. They cover an extraordinary range of poetic influences scattered throughout the history of the West. We seldom think how strange it is that in the modern world, with its vast archaeological scholarship, and its editing of almost every significant work of literature ever written, however obscure the language (from Frobenius's translations of African folktales to Robert Bringhurst's translations of the Haida epic poet, Skaay), poets, visual artists, and musicians have the whole extent of known history before them. They can choose at will from it. A contemporary artist in Paris can step into the Musée du quai Branly to find inspiration in Australian aboriginal art, which only half a century ago was as remote from the West as any art could possibly be. The same is true for contemporary musicians, who can choose from the music of the world — and in the same museum, which has extensive ethnographic music collections. "World music" is now the name of a musical style.

Any poet with a good university library (and Hart has spent years in them) has all the poetry of the past at his disposal with a rapidity that is disconcerting if one cares at all for poetry as the product of a place, having, like wine, distinctive qualities produced by local soil and climate. Nowadays, art is always rushing off for its influences and for its inspiration to somewhere else, somewhere formerly far. In such circumstances, having roots is an encumbrance, limiting one's range and certainly one's speed. Hart's poems range widely and in some of the sequences are amazingly swift, succinct for speed, as Milton says. They are never in one place but often in all places, and this is what makes them at times so unsettling, and so contemporary. It is not his erudition, which is deep but worn lightly, that unsettles. It is the sense of speed. He can go anywhere, fast, and the reader has to keep up. The effect is dizzying, for him as well as us. We try to find our feet.

The exhilaration may be worth it, but the exhaustion of being everywhere at once tells. This is not an aesthetic criticism of the poems but an account of how they tell us what it feels like to be, in our time, so unnaturally aware of the past. So, in *Dream Salvage*, after a horrifying but exhilarating poem on Caesar's wars, with the faces of Caesar's troops bespattered with the blood of their Germanic enemies, who are dying "like massacred bison," Hart writes of lying awake at night, his sheets soaked with sweat, thinking of such events by the thousand, in "the confusion of time / misplaced," asking "why these / fragments [the very word is a famous fragment from Eliot] haunt / why these ancient wars in the ruin of an after-time?" The poet feels the burden of our exceptional and, as I said, unnatural and fragmentary knowledge of the past as an excuse for our own fragmentation, an imagined cause, "invented after, the wind / At my back." But perhaps our vast, rootless knowledge, our ability to travel so far and so widely in the past, our "confusion of time," is the true cause of our fragmentation. The wind is in our face.

The intellectual and spiritual project of these books is carried forward in *Dreamwork* (2010), with its more open acknowledgement of what Hart calls "the pathology of a time we call history." Those of us who teach complain that students no longer care about history. Is it possible they, and we, care too much for the content of history while obliterating time, the time of the setting sun as continuous with the time of the decline of an empire? This thought may be lodged in the meaning of the lapidary lines, "A life that asks too many questions / Is like one that asks too few / A nightmare."

A splendid, chewy, Anglo-Saxon sound is heard in these poems, evoking twentieth-century horrors: "The crushed rock mounts against the chain-link fence / The coils of barbed wire line the top rung." It is a splendid sound, and a horrible memory. But it is not the death camps that are being directly described, although they are evoked. It is the rail line outside Newark, New Jersey, juxtaposed to the razor wire one sees incongruously and brutally on the college walls at the University of Cambridge. Cambridge recalls Spenser and Marlowe, among others, evoking the verse of the Elizabethan age, and even Spenser's pastoral verse is now seen by us, from our vantage in the future, as if through concentration-camp wire.

Musing, the book presented here, is unexpectedly a book of sonnets, another Elizabethan form. Given the nature of that form, it is hard to speak generally of a series such as this in terms that accord it the praise it deserves, except to say that these poems — 109 of them — are technically impressive, imaginatively resourceful, wide ranging, and often, in the peculiarly detached way I have described as unfolding in the earlier books, emotionally moving. Inevitably, a series of sonnets of this length invites comparison of some kind with the greatest series of sonnets ever written, Shakespeare's, but in this case the comparison draws attention first to their difference thematically. Illustrating the difference between our time and all others, that is, the hypertrophied availability to us of the material remains of the past, these sonnets range far and wide over historical time and space.

After Shakespeare, whose sonnets are concerned almost exclusively with love and time (though he finds astonishing variety in these themes), the possibilities of the sonnet were considerably expanded, especially by Milton and Wordsworth, the former making the sonnet a political form, the latter a means of theological reflection, among other things. To the reader attuned to such subtleties, Hart's poems show continual awareness of the history of the sonnet form, and especially of the place and time of their origin with Petrarch at Avignon, in the south of France. But Hart's sonnets do something remarkable with the form, which is consonant with all his poetry to date. Unlike Milton or Wordsworth, Hart retains the original thematic core of the sonnet as a love poem, and the many comments on love in them are deeply moving. Yet even as Hart reaches back to the origin of the sonnet, he pushes the form down into a layered reflection on history and the world, from Greek and Phoenician traders to the present.

I have said that Hart has traveled widely and thought deeply about the places he has been. As his diction reveals, he possesses in memory the poets who have written of those places. Chinese poetry, perhaps Li Po, is recalled in the final verse, "the river is our breath," though the river in question is the Seine. The line "In Provence far from the snows of then" recalls one of the great lines of medieval French poetry, by François Villon, lamenting the beautiful, proud ladies celebrated in Provençal verse, who disappear like snow before the sun: "Où sont les neiges d'antan?" The poems resonate throughout, as very good poems do, with the sounds of other and earlier voices in song. Sappho is delightfully captured and parodied — though the humour is deliberately at the author's expense — in the following poem, which conflates her song of blinding passion with her sadly ironic reflection on age:

> My eyes dim, my desire
> Unabated gets lost on the way. This
>
> Tongue stumbles into the tyranny of thorns
> And the surfaces condemn me to be
> Alone: death — rude, savage, cruel — empties me
> And leaves me to waste by the road I once
>
> Strode along when I was young. Youth is never
> Wasted: there's just not enough of it.
> No one wants a dry repose: the music
> Seems sadder now. There's nothing to be done.

From the outset, it is clear Hart expands the formal possibilities of the sonnet, using a looser rhyme scheme balanced by the final, Shakespearean couplet. But soon even this level of adherence to the traditional form is loosened and a wider, more flexible range of structures obtains within the fourteen-line form. In one instance (sonnets 73 and 74) a sentence crosses over from one poem into the next. All these technical innovations are happy, giving the series variety and avoiding the occasional monotony of even the best sonnet series. Sonnet 48 is an *ars poetica*, in which Hart states fairly clearly his own expectations of the form, and its challenges.

One thing the sonnet was made to do, although this has not always been apparent to poets who write them, is to deliver lapidary observations. Hart does this time and again, for example, in the second sonnet, "Time happens to other / People," or in the fourth, "children being what we were and might have been." Also, "When I was young the world was young: you know / The rest"; "The dead stacked up like wood"; "The crumbling mill, the soul"; "The ineffable / Unthing that is us." There are many other examples.

The final sonnet, on Paris, is a beautiful example of what I see throughout this collection, which is a mind typically Canadian. It is also a mind deeply educated in European history and culture, but contemplating European history and culture from a uniquely Canadian, paradoxical point of view. The

European past is us, and it is not us, and the more we go to Europe, or even to the United States, away from ourselves, so to speak, the stronger this sense of marriage and separation is. That fissure in our lives is re-expressed in this last poem, which is set in Paris. It is the speaker's separation from the addressee, the loved one, and this separation calls up the most famous of separated lovers, Héloïse and Abelard. The speaker knows the very streets (the tangled warren around the church of Saint Julien le Pauvre, on the left bank of the Seine, just opposite Notre Dame), where Héloïse and Abelard loved. These are the very few medieval streets that were not bulldozed and overlaid with avenues in the nineteenth century by the great city planner, Georges-Eugène Haussmann. A personal, erotic separation becomes Paris's separation from its medieval past, which resonates with the separation of the North American consciousness from its European origin. This separation is alluded to by the erasure of the history of Paris by Haussmann's straight avenues — which are beautiful but not nurturing of love's obliquities. In the end, the elaborate urban comparison seems about to collapse, until the river Seine returns, with its natural obliquities. However

much the city changes, the river is the same, and is
like the breath of life:

The barges slip along the Seine, the wind has died
By Notre Dame: the heat of August burns the stone
Even as the night has come. The winter of our hearts

Is gone, and your absence here is the only
Way this city lacks. The moon is snow
Over the Sorbonne, the voice of Héloïse

Fleeing down the few crooked streets Haussmann left.
The avenues are gorgeous, but love is seldom
Linear. It would be folly to lose

Paris or you to metaphor. At Christmas
We will come here and watch the shadows
Between the ruined trees and remember.

Love is in the place and feels the types
Words might make: the river is our breath.

These deeply thoughtful poems bring layered his-
torical consciousness into the sonnet. They also
touch and stir the heart through all its levels.

Gordon Teskey
4 May 2010

musing

1.

The boughs lay withered beyond the brow
The village hung in the hollow, unseen
As your hand that night, the moon
A reflection of that lapse, the copse
And bower hidden down the lane, now
Your flesh, the blush of a plum
Caught the sun as it slipped, the yard
In bloom as dusk hushed the orchard
And the search of darkness was almost
Upon us: it leaves an old man breathless
To feel all that again, even as a distant
Aftermath, the harvest already done.
The marrow simmers and shivers long past the time
When young blood thrills at the April wind.

2.

What is not said in the garden
The roses could almost hear, the whisper
Of thorns caught our hearts like a limb
Awry, unable to make the stile, the meadows
Stretching down to the river, the ghosts
Of war poets, murmuring of love, haunt
The hedges and the pub. The darkness
Of December remains a trace, the years
Have run from our bones and we would not
Believe it until it happened. These fingers
Are stiff with time and the mind stunned
That it would be thus. Time happens to other
People, bent out of shape like a pear tree
In a gale: beyond the wall you speak still.

The sparrow on the trough is world enough
As bright as any cardinal: it cannot swoop
Like a barnswallow, cannot glide like a gull,
Is not as exalted as a dove. It's strange
How birds become signs in the mind, how they
Are projections of ideology,
Of love, riding the wind beyond ink,
Never left to their own devices. In writing
Of you, small, brown and plain, I feel the guilt
Of misrepresentation, not allowing you to be
As you are, to yourself and nature, a little
Like a poet writing to his love of his love.
Pictures and similitudes shroud the eye
That is a mirror that cannot see itself.

4.

The garden in the ruined abbey brims
With lovers, the voices of Dane, Viking,
Tudor faint beyond the choir, choristers
Practising within the walls. The roses
Recall the dead airmen, the trees reaching
Over the stream. You used to play here
And still do. Windows of the night curtain
The pavement at nightfall, and I dreamt
That time reversed itself and we were going
Back, although nothing could be the same,
And I wondered whether second chances
Were lost causes. The sun falls on the walk
As if it were the moon, the laughter
Of children being what we were and might have been.

5.

Your face was the chalk in these hills
The rain galloping on the metal roof
The wind from the sea shaking our windows
That was seven years ago now: our bones
Live in the land but not quite. You are still
Lovely though a bit stooped: my eyes cannot see
Matter — lovers have souls even though
Satires and the tabloids have it right
Some of the time. The water pounds down through the trough
And drowns out pomposity. I began
To speak about love: the moon yawns over the gate
And you sleep with your thoughts. There I will err
In describing the bond that frees in this storm.

6.

The fen stretches out like prairie, the canals
And dikes are more linear than love,
The geometry of desire would shame
The poet into exile, love far
From empire. The cathedral surveys
The land, once a lake, and you look over
The pasture and see something else. You record
Your own lines: your toes feel the mud, the wind
Cooling them from the scorch of day. What
I cannot see grows each day, shadows extend
On the faces we pass. The small of your back
Moves like a wave and gathers its own
Invisible shore. We walk where boats once fled
Armies chasing the death of time like love itself.

7.

They married looking out to sea, the west
Storm, cloud, horizon: the church is now
A trust, the Celtic names of Cornwall buried
In the yard. Your mother's people left
This green for another, but the place
They abandoned — there was no going back —
Was not as it is. The land remains but not
The leases, the hunger and diseases I imagine.
There is a history to love, facts that slip
Between the sheets, material to build a day,
A life, that poets forget. We see the lovely
Cliffs at Morwenstow without the motives
That took them out to sea. These lovers were
Phoenicians wandering with and without tin.

8.

All from the stars the shards fell, light condensed
In leaves circling the earth, and we, condemned,
Faced the dying sun, the night of our curse
Leaving us for dead. Your eyes were the end

The sun winding up so long after
No one was there to remember, the voice
Too sure in its claims, omniscience
A dream played in physics and poetry

Sometimes in love. It's hard not to get
Lost in the animal, to make this flesh
Vegetable, to whisper in your ear
What might have been, the day the garden fell.

In the suburbs of our affections we see
Bones and shadows that we want to be.

9.

The winter of our breath was the blue
Of the sky, the sound of our feet
On the crust was a crisp horizon,
The taste of your tears was salt, the sea

Extending like your arms to the hill. Time
Has come between us: there are not enough
Lives to live. Blood and marrow age
Almost unnoticed until dusk is falling

Bombs splintering home, child, street. What love
Grows amid the rubble, how do we return
To the silence by the shore, sublimate
The noise that distracts us from what matters?

This life sentence demands the mending
Of exile, healing the scar, the winding.

10.

So the wind was on your sleeve: you asked me
Questions I could not answer. The metaphysics
Of love was lost in the detail of a child's gaze
His look aground, the size of crickets, the leap

Of a frog. We look at the sky and he inquires
After lake bottom and forest floor. I
Chase abstractions like butterflies, but he
Knows those wings are real, that doubt creeps in

For those who don't look close enough. You sense
Something we don't and so does she, a child
His age, who considers how all of us speak
At angles to each other, how the wind

Winds us at different rates. But she is not
Putting a spin on whether love is hot.

11.

Taboo in the stem of my skull, the danger
I make for myself, or would, instinct
In dreams askance in day or night, bleeds
The light at the end of my fingers, wastes

The songs I might make for the young. The clay
I would shape with touch and justice would melt
In the rain that drives out the sun, the pledge
I gave that day I first spoke. The way

Gives way: rules — each has its prison —
Mazes that exchange precepts for breath. This ghost
Smothers this soul, these bones, a fiction
That can work up a sweat. Dreams matter.

Some urge, some turn, you will plead and coax
The sting of flesh, the mind, is no hoax.

12.

You sang, black Madonna, your breasts more perfect
Than dogma, your lush smile more fertile
Than the Nile, the symmetry of your thought
More astonishing than the pyramids.

Let us compare not geometries but myths
We elaborate from our marrow, the stones
We kick from our shoes, the marvel we find
From that child, the one who peers from your lap

Through a space vaster than time that seems
Close and immediate, and you vanish
Like the woman on the train at New Brunswick
Gorgeous against all injustice and laws.

How can your canvas be flesh, your gaze
From old paint miles away be her, here, these days?

13.

The cusp of the dark falls on Central Park
And your face, as if we never met, alight,
Your son in the stroller, a stranger,
And only in my mind there is more.

I have named a place in a song
And made the ripple of words drift
Against convention. I imagine a love
Without stain or boils: no wrong

Have I done you, woman, passerby.
I have no curious dreams where I name you
A character. You are, nameless to me, more
To those you know than any poem can say.

This poet, poem, gets lost on Fifth Avenue
And you live on this earth on your own terms.

14.

Breath, too, can plummet, magic rougher
Than the stars, the sun in the azure
I remember from the morning: you were
Mutinous that nature would winter

Our bones, flatten us like some ridiculous
Rhyme or run-on line youth had turned
In the face of age. I am struck with dumb
Stillness in the wood: here our breath

Is a clear fog in the clean air, our fears
Hear our hearts in our breath, the oaks
Shooting in the leaf-dazzle of autumn
And a storm is around the corner.

Their words are gorse and thorn our hearts
In the day-night of the confusion we parse.

15.

The aspersion she cast cuts deep: the times
Wind down like theories built on algebra
And Hymen sleeps in mythology
Tired, perhaps oblivious, to graphs and curves

Charting the decline of the bed strewn with flowers
The wedding torches have gone smoky
And the vexation of the spirit and flesh
Divorces hand and eye. Hormones rage

Against the dying light, there but unnamed
To our ancestors. A maze of rules governs
The ungovernable, but we have
Our names still. Some words are knives.

She would burn my words with her breath
Her truth lying where it most protests.

16.

Impostors shape fictions of marrow and soul
The light subdues you but not really
Vineyards are commonwealths, and love knows
Its contraries: your eyes express

Their own political philosophy. The tide
Ebbs, our blood with it. Our lips must reach
Beyond politics, but, if not, then let
Them be moist and hot. Let this

Triviality keep the baleful from ruling,
Wearing, burning lovers, strangers, strays.
This is our prayer, the three thieves hanging
On a hill: we all pretend to virtue.

Some say Cressida died yesterday by the wall
Whose ashes players smeared on their faces.

17.

Son, you were allergic to filberts then
And the moon on my Inuit shirt
Was more than an artificial paradise.
The flâneurs in the park would stare

At the Finnish jackets you and your sister
Wore all those years, which, like Niagara
Poured like our blood in the riverrun.
It's hard to speak of love to a child

On the verge, you will shape and speak
Your changes, think, perhaps that girls
Make the world worth something. Your poems
Were real from the first: you shook

The neck of rhetoric and threw it out
And taught my heart with your first shout.

18.

Daughter, you are more delicate
Than any of my words, you quicken me
And keep me from gloom. You stride this side
Of being a woman and calling the world,

I hope, your own. When I saw you rise up
From the womb, thrashing, wide-eyed, moving
Your limbs with intelligence
I knew I could teach you nothing

But might be your guide this side
Of paradise. What can I say
About love when time has changed
And you will have a world to invent?

I hear your wit as I fade in the wood
And the limbs of the gods have turned to leaves.

19.

Vexation burned when the sun beat on the waves
And no matter how much I looked away
I was blinded, saw your face rise like a sword,
The dead king sent out on a barrow

To drift into mythology,
A dream in and out of consciousness
And the smell of cedar in my nostrils still
Lodged by the lake. On the other side

Beyond the bay, the four great smokestacks rose
On the shore changing utterly your hair
The texture of poetry: the oak and earth
Turned on themselves and love was barely

Possible. It is hard amid affliction
For roses to bud and lips to touch.

20.

The tongue is spare: the wind lifts on the dirt road
The wild strawberries hang by the gate. Dust
Clings to her thighs, the rain still on her clothes.

Memory seeps in the gravel: the geese
Squawk by the shore, rise and vee high in the sky
And vanish like a friend strewn in the years.

She might be pausing on him in her haste
But probably not. He would lie on the dock
And sway to the waves, look her way askance

And say nothing. She could feel his imagined gaze
On the small of her back: she was surprised
At her cool moist lips. Time could not do that.

21.

This harvest is the sap that moves in us,
Rose, maple, our lust and thoughts arise
From the seasons. Tonight spring is in your eyes

And your soul comes from the juices of flowers
Pine, crabapple, cedar all scented your hair
Draped and raised the wind shaking the trees.

You have risen from the forest floor
And my fingers are ivy that run:
The deer hiding in the brush. This cannot be

And seems as ludicrous as goddesses
And gods shifting, transforming, shovelling
Coal in a dream like a steam engine.

22.

The dog beyond the gate barked, as if
Human love were strange, like the silent whistle

Dogs only can hear. You know how desperate
I am when cats stray into a sonnet.

The human zoo is nothing like the sun
And the ethnology of lust gets lost

In cannibals and Amazons, the threats
To flesh, the anguish. Love becomes

A territory of unrequited dreams.
Your eyes gaze out from the porch

And the sun is growing dim by the rail.
It is late, and in this town they are born

And die. It's like that. The wind blows on your coffee,
Spills it, and no one is there to lap it.

23.

If joy could screeve from lung and marrow
And love could exsect sorrow from the blood
I could watch the snow on the cardinal
As it was, not as a sign of something else.

Years indurate the mind, thoughts stone, the rain
Gall to our dance, when young, we would sing
Not golem then, and crooch by the shore
The fire the night missed with the moon.

There was something comic: she said they would
Bummel, less graceful than deer, ideas
Big-footed as clowns, the paronomasia
Of love poetry playing with sound.

I cut my knuckle on a thorn, not words,
And the rails were asymptotes of desire.

24.

You sculch my secret signs, as though I illude
The shadows by the barn door, the crow hoarse
From warning me, nothing apparent here
In the hieratic ode of faded oak.

The red paint is a metaphor for the rose
That was once the blood of love, enfolded,
A coat to weather the tempests, the feelings
That go into a kiss or all those years.

And the hiatus between flesh and soul,
The almost there of wishes and remorse,
You and I would be a we, together, divided,
Heartsore, headstrong, down and out in love.

Words are whispers that curve in the wind,
Love hopes, a creed, crestfallen, rising.

25.

The scree on the beach was lost in your breath
The sand on the ink began to dry
And form a world between art and life.

While the wind blew and changed change itself
And the birch hung over the lake, its leaves
Turning on the dark water, you turned

And watched the light on the train flicker
Down the line like memory, the taste
Of wild raspberries tart on your lips.

And the sun is set deep in your mind,
The voices of strangers in the wood, this place
Where I cannot return for fear of ruin.

In time the land is paved and broken
And the beach bleeds an ink like oil.

26.

The renitency of the will opposes all
In love, the moon on the marsh is awash
In the dark of the winter sky, and your eyes

Are orbs, animated in ways surmised.
The dust on your hands is not snow
But has the same hue: the wistful pull

Of desire is like perpetual exile.
The leaves hang on the bare limbs
In the wood, and the deer hide in the hollow.

The years have passed, almost unnoticed
And we, with a certain stubbornness, have gone
With breath itself into the dark, our pulses

Quickened but numb to the buffets, the wind
A dream like the whisper across our faces.

27.

The sea scrubs the rock, the clouds on the cape
Hang, the water swelling, ashimmer,
Sun, high over Africa, blinds even over
The white sky: you sit looking out

Your sweater cumulus, your hair filaments,
The wine as golden. The dogs frolic, chase, laze
As only the Midi can afford them.
The crowds from the Calanques muster

Into the port. The woman next to us
Has lips swollen from collagen
For reasons only her biographer knows
Or those who set the standards for films.

She does not need that, Ariadne left
Amid the maze of cafés: you, I speechless.

28.

The turquoise water is not faked on a postcard.
The deliverance of the sea in the dying light
Is not something poets surmise. Winds here

Can be hot in January. No sirens rise
From the reefs: the boats, in rows,
Sit in the cove as if storms never were.

Love in the marrow, no matter how
Embarrassing a word can be, manifests
Itself in heat and light, bone and vessel

And rises and falls at first and last light.
The older I get, the less I know. You have
Made your way, son, up another cliff.

Those Greek and Phoenician traders knew many signs
For love: it is not just the heat of the blood.

29.

The windows of the moon have cast
What was and might have been at once

And the dreams of our helixes hold
Something before and after us, the moist

Whisper of those of us we could not
And will not know. Love in the shadows

Of what they suspected, what we surmise
Leads us along, the oak and pine drinking

From the sand. Why others have disciplined
Those whose guesses are different, codes

To chase away chaos, God only knows
But they will take it up for That cause.

It's hard to turn to the warm of your hand,
Daughter, as we speak in a tongue they fled.

30.

They were quartering us in these streets
Those centuries ago, and we hung on

To this tongue for long, but haltingly,
Like love itself, we try to get along

And make sounds that are as naked
As Eden. At night we all chase

Separate desires and meet in day
To try to muddle amid the penumbra

Making couplets of the great heave
Of breath and dust, the moon on our shoes

And creatures within us far more ancient
Than humans, les roches a different kind

Of love story. Plants all atrample;
The animals flee before our terror.

31.

There was a window on the stars, the cusp
Of the bay caught the curve of your neck
And the boats caught the sun in repetition,
Heaving on the waves like youth in heat:
It wasn't elegant, and some barn
In a memory — it could have been in Somerset
Or another leaning in the Gatineau — eclipsed
The sun in Provence, forgetting Petrarch.

That kind of plank will not do in poetry
A cove is not a cave, a poet not a farmer.
The tired sublimity of words refuses
To make love an eclogue, to hoe laurel.
No matter what the troubadours said
Love, knowing absence, is in heart as much as head.

32.

Keel, mast, sail in wind, sea, sky shake and bend
As if to till the swell, and Circe calling
As the brides weep for those lost. The dead
Moan over the koan-cropped waves, falling

A myth as enfolded as flesh. Aphrodite
Bears no rhyme, no grudge on the edge
Of the sea. Only the cliff is wine red
And the water is a metaphor for blood.

And there you were as if the outcrop
Were a bow thrust in the cusp, your face
Pelted with spume, the fish thick and shimmering
Dance sunward, your voice trailing off

Like the present. The almonds are in blossom
And this winter barely chills the marrow.

33.

Her pale hair stumbled in the wood, and he rode
To see her singing by a tree, the loam

On her feet deep and red. It was her hair
That made her fall and sit, the light

From the sea nipping her heart. And so
Many wars started over lust by a bough

Or the march from Spain along the sea
And the chansons, even with vestiges

Of England, Normandy and Aquitaine,
Wafted over the swords on to the waves.

She would not recognize herself here,
The ghosts climbing the winding stair, and might

Write another song to counter this bronze
And beauty of the empire fallen.

34.

There was jazz playing in a room away
And the lit margin of the hill rippled
In the night, and the dead chapel

Ruined on a cliff felt like dust.
Dionysius blew his horn till dawn
And the madness of midsummer had come

Nothing was really predictable
Ever, the secrets of love and state
Rifted over the rocks of the port. The winds

Blew off Africa: all the goats had gone
And the vineyards looked like graveyards
And empires, like lovers, slipped away.

In time blood and drum pound, the space of light
Casting across your neck as you sing.

35.

The winds rise over the plain outside Paris
The sun bounces off the cranes, buildings
Crop from the broken earth, ancient battles
Erased from the land. Her eyes once gazed
Over the hedges before the imported palms
The lovers on the train oblivious.

Was it the first as France grew from island
To empire, a woman at the centre, and she
In verse, wood, stone a monument, as though?
The heat of her lips, the blood of the cross
Confused the blush that time has left us,
And later Petrarch, finding refuge
In Avignon, wrote. What of your voice, touch,
Left behind on the platform at Crécy?

36.

Till we fled Calais these two terrains
Were joined, Normandy and Paris at odds,
Thoughts of love between battles, even as we died
Between dynasties. Passing a gymnasium
Named after Descartes, through callow birch,
I find it hard to imagine stripping all down
To ego, to logic in a chimney,
To the difference between estat and estate.

Where does love make its way between abstraction
And ammunition? Those words are so fleet-footed
Spilling over, putting pressure on four letters
As if. Amorous nights in a wasteful
Brevity cannot be bridled
In a syllogism: and your hair.

37.

Window night–frame
The rust of these knuckles
Alludes, the salt
Of tongue elides, denies

A lover of broken tithes.
Graffiti score the route
The passengers alone
With their thoughts

Dreams of fire
Collide with a weariness
That leads to death.
I cannot know

You I have lived with
All the days.

time of the moon
I write my own tune
nothing equilateral
my dress in bloom.

you have your rituals
to keep you in clothes
to sing you to sleep
the touch of the rose

at the fold of my blouse
in the feel of my paint
the taste of my sorrow
is found in my print

and the bold of your hand
vanishes with magic.

38.

I have washed too many
dishes and clothes
wool, porcelain, iron
have rubbed me

I have watched
the moon turn
to blood, kicked stones
on empty roads

the wrong way. My children
I have bathed in tub, lake,
sea, and have sung
them to sleep in fever

crossed purposes like swords
cut myself on thorns,
briars, basilisks
and sought you

I have walled up late
when you should have
been home, dug in the soil
with hands too rough

in the market. While others
swilled, I waited
to return to you,
your hair lavender

for their years. I even played
violin when you died

as the sun climbed
over the vacant field

39.

There were stones   there were knives
        the window opened
Out on the moon   to the sun
        the houselights
Shone on the river   shimmered on the ripple.

The winter garden   grew a snow
        almost green
And the noise   of mobile phones
        disturbed it
And the quiet   of poetry. And so

The buzz of filler   became
        a found art
And I found myself   filled
        with a vacant heart.

40.

It's not custom to begin with the couplet
As if love were something contained in a sonnet

No one has figured out how to convert breath
To flesh, to make profession action
And to hear in the silence of the loved
Defiance of all representation.

I can't pretend to know how to arrange
Words and life in lines like rows of stones
The battles have left, or to count the rain
Like the tears of lovers left or in time

Bereft of what was sure. These plots are too gross
For the pain they felt along the way
And the whisper they caught on the walk
But it's some kind of trace no matter how pale.

41.

The angles of the moon over, through those trees,
Ochre, pearl, bleach, cast in Princeton
Not far from battlefield and graveyard,
The Revolution no longer counted

In months. People of different crafts
And colours are buried here, saw something
Like this. Their blood moved like the tides
And the windows of the sun cast

Its reflection, its face on the water,
The surprise of deer in the dark wood, over
Three hundred shot, culled, felled
By a theory of conservation, the smell

Of gunsmoke like the myth it left
Behind the dream the moon might have been.

42.

The absence of your breath heats my marrow
As impossible as that might be: touch
Has a history of its own. Your hair

Will outlast stone. The dream of speech
The breeze on the leaves, the voices
Of our children in my brain, like a great

Code, a music and score wired into the soul
That word stuns modernity like Mao's
Gun barrel. How do we estimate

The children we were and take the distance
We are, apart, and not be wistful?
The almond trees will be blooming

In Provence far from the snows of then
As they cut our ankles in the north wind.

43.

The embarrassment of words abandons us
To the world, traces when breath and taste

Are gone. We scratch out signs to leave,
Archive, shard, sigh, footnote, plea,

The dust on our heads after. Words never
Quite arrive like flesh itself, and life

Sheds like the tides a kind of accident,
A debris, ashes. Then first and last words,

Literally and not, begin to forget
Their speakers. I don't remember what

Noise I first made and will not recall
The final syllables. Words are fictions

But breath and your eyes, son, are as real
As the earth, the sky, the puzzlement.

44.

The hawthorn trembles in rain and ice
The peril of exile on my head
As you walk in the orchard, the squander

Of sun spread on the water, and the wind
Scatters these words: neither cares about
Courtly love. That is quaint beside the rubble,

The dead stacked up like wood. The poets lie
Between truth and lies, the scent of roses
Cuts the nose like a thorn. Those eyes gaze

At the pond where Narcissus fell, a servant
To a kind of love that hides behind claims
To a love far greater. The hills breathe with snow

And the Midi sun burns off its accident
And I yearn for a touch that will not dissolve.

45.

Just when it seems she will sing deport
From some ancient Occitan love poem
And desire will win the day, the song
Of the hour leads these lovers down
Some incomprehensible garden path
That even the ghost of Petrarch cannot
Follow, and in the meadows he complains
About soldiers of Islam, coming from

Africa. The old names of love and war
Are as anxious as lovers asleep on a bed
Of newspapers with screaming headlines
About clashes in the suburbs
In the Middle East. The wind blows sand
On the prints that vanish with their breath.

46.

Through the threshold the pollen draws, the light
A hinge opening out on to the blue
Shimmer, the water stretching past the cliff
To Africa. The refuge of your face,
With your absence, takes up my brain
And casts it on the wind. The tangle

Of whatever makes me not so visible,
Awakens to the distance, the thenness
Of air, to the solitary walk
We take to our graves. With each year
I know the veil more through touch and smell,
The everyday. Abstractions and great systems
Grow more empty — drums and hoops taper off
To the vanishing point: your voice in the yard.

47.

And yet the morning light held you, the cuts
Of age not healing any time soon
On me, the worn iniquity, beauty

Fading like paint in the sun. Time choked me
As I slept, throttled the rose on the ledge,
Gouged the old man's eyes, bent truth

Like so much tin. But the sweat was real
And you were there when I awoke, and terror
Stayed long into the light. Life makes

And moves these bones until the yard takes them back
No enmity against time prevails, the weeds
Surmount us even as the poetry of dust.

Yet your hair in the sun leads to your eyes
And while living against odds we seek no lies.

48.

When I was young the world was young: you know
The rest. Instead of making more sense
The world makes less. My eyes dim, my desire
Unabated gets lost on the way. This

Tongue stumbles into the tyranny of thorns
And the surfaces condemn me to be
Alone: death — rude, savage, cruel — empties me
And leaves me to waste by the road I once

Strode along, when I was young. Youth is never
Wasted: there's just not enough of it.
No one wants a dry repose: the music
Seems sadder now. There's nothing to be done.

If this pen could pause, and turn back the tide,
I'd never say again that time had lied.

49.

It would be as the wind, but some force
Within, disdainful and inglorious, pries
These lids shut, the living laughing
At the dead, for now. What is the slow dark
That moves in me, extinguishing the sun
And folding the blood in on itself?

I am mortgaged to the slander
Of an ill, vague and evasive mouth, pulling
The heart like refuse, and casting
The bones in vexation. No oath will endure
The breach of sand cast by a dry wind.

It does no good to brood on the wilt of time
But in the heart so random this thing.

50.

This night, like the vanity of death,
Lays me down, a ghost on the street,
With false subtlety, the habit of trust
Cast, garbage to the skies: the stench
Of plague is no memory here.

Despair is no spirit now. Hours
Are sold to treachery, yet the scent
Of the almond trees makes indignation
Seem excessive. Love swears even
Among the false. You would not lie

For comfort or advantage. Smell the wind
From your window. If you speak untrue
Then the world is lost. I will leave
Expectations and dip my feet in the sea.

51.

Palm trees came to France in 1864
And so were not with Petrarch at Avignon.
They are a new kind of love plant: time shifts
Even for poets and lovers. The mad
Are aware of so much we are not:
They do not fret over the same conventions.

They are not sure Laura is your name
Or the one they would choose whether your eyes
Were not like the sun. They have no bias
Against colour, and blonde is just one
Option. Often they have more to worry about —
Their next meal, for instance. Dreams
For them are armies of the night: they fear
Drugs and involuntary incarceration.

Some have seen angels and have known love.

52.

Freezing to death is not an act of love
Or any effect love might have: greed, like lust,
Knows no bounds. Budgets, like lovers, can be
Illicit and rationalize what you never thought
Could be. Beggars have desires, and gypsies
Have nostrils to smell, and scapegoats
Sing in choirs that angels might flock to
If they had not been placed and misplaced.

In some corner of that garden, perhaps
By the wall, I wish love would have no
Politics, would not need the law to sort
It out when the fruit went bad in the windfall.
Beds have revenues and rents but might hold
Roses, or lilies that would not fester.

53.

Your arms are not a trope, and hyperbole
Would hang me just as well. Mobs do not write
Love poetry, and greeting cards try too hard,
And shards and slivers make swift dispatch.

Art is cruel when youth and beauty flees
And dogs grow testy amid ticks and fleas
While oblivion razes the guard of satire.

Tempests might bend us in the compass
Of an hour and sand might leave us
Like a ruin, but love, as embarrassing
As it sounds, will prove and stay. That does not

Mean that it will come with ease: au contraire
It will endure — these lines are not your hair.

54.

Flint, outcrop, overhang: I made my way
Over the stone outlay thrust up
Before there were eyes to see. Lyell
And Darwin wrote odes to geology

And the love of birds and archipelago
Before I was born or knew who they were.
I was a child who ran along the shore
Of a glacial lake, climbed through the forest

On some of the most ancient and worn hills
In the world. When I left that land of flies
And bugs that burst in the sudden summer,
I lost my way in a labyrinth of rules.

Sand was not textual for me then, and now
I look back, for love, through shards and measures.

55.

So much depends on the glibness of words,
Sounds of love, professions of the absurd.

That is the trouble when we end in a couplet
The messiness of breath, the spilling over
Of lush bushes on the almost ruined castle
On the Rhône, we always miss the point.

We are always working backward, missing the present,
Thoughts of the future eaten by the past
Before we ever arrive. It's a little like life
And a love poem: you could do better

But won't try. That gives me pause, why I bother
When other hands could hold forth. In time
We all limp, the finish line vanishing
Before us, erotic visions agape.

56.

I am not certain: je ne suis pas sûr
Qu'est-ce que la langue d'amour
Translations on the railway walls
Industrial scars or art, some rendez-vous,
La dolce vita gone awry after five
On a Friday night. The rail line cuts
Through Avignon where Petrarch cast about
For ways to change the way people talked

About love, perhaps even lived. Popes
Held court here when trains were fictions
And the Polish monk had not yet demoted
The earth. The red bauxite is
Lovers' blood even as it transforms.

57.

When Venus moved her headquarters, she sighed
And took a second, called out Paris
In answer to some other question
Regarding Helen and Homer, maybe
Some arcane pursuit of the oral
Tradition, proofs of authorship, blind
Tests, but, being the goddess of love,

She got to decide where the fashion houses
Would form and what were the laws of perfume.
Provence could no longer sustain what
Greece had begun, in myth at least.
Exhausted by subordinate clauses, she got down
To business, warned Cupid never to end
Another sonnet sequence: time to get real.

58.

The closer to the ground, the more fictional
the syllogism: the TGV is not unlike
those Canterbury tales. M&Ms, Pepsi

two men taking over my table, swilling
mouths agape, occupying space, as if pleasure
weren't enough and they wanted me to leave.

One speaks of Dijon, the other plays with his
earphones, the SONY tapes advertising
love itself: degustation, and out

the window a crane. Lovers at right angles
to apartment blocks. It would be tempting
to hear one more story from the Wife of Bath.

Along the roads people move in their cars
Alone with their silent prayers to commerce.

59.

Silent devotion at first light, wind
Breath on the ankles, the frost in the stone
Numb to the touch. The canticles of loss

Are buried with the revolution. That love
Couldn't be left alone, even if they are
Traces in the noise and smoke of a world

More given to deafness and poison.
It was always hard on the knees to pray,
Harder to do when eye and brain wandered

Errant, truant, spent before the sun
Would rise and raze the shaky steeple,
The crumbling mill, the soul. And so as I go

To Paris, I wonder whether the monks would take me
For a retreat in and from the city I love.

60.

Those catacombs, stacked with skulls and bones
For over two hundred years, where the Resistance
Hid as the Nazis ruled Paris, are they places
For poetry or an inventory the heart

Can't abide? The green near Lyon
Is gaudy beside the dry Midi
I left behind. How does rain affect

The way we bury the dead? Masses
Of the living, their absent traces
Yet so palpable even when the songs

They sang their children are long gone.
Time has disembodied them, and poets
And lovers are not exempt, even
As their words seem to dance for a while longer.

61.

The way trains move, poetry moves
Or trains move me to poetry: this isn't
An idle claim but has been true since

I can remember. How we move is like sap
Or wind, depending, and words that move
Need care for the reader. This train slaps

Along the track, sometimes it is air
And the ears fill and void as on a flight.
Lovers are trains — we were like a train

And although youth. I'll stop there:
To get to the bottom of things is not
To depress. We pass through a flooded wood
The symmetry of leafless trees still, reflecting
Various shades of the sky in and of themselves.

62.

I have a whole cache I will one day
Find and it will give another story,
No second Troy, but, until then,

I will have to make do with desire
And memory as I glide across the great
Northern plain. Allusion is much

Less dangerous than a kiss. Vows will seem
As quaint as love itself, for the divergence
Of the twain, and the multiplicity

Of eros, become this time. Words are
Some kind of evidence if love exists
And is evident. You shake with a laughter

That responds to insubstantial words:
Perhaps love is as absurd as grammar.

63.

You see before you a man more ridiculous
Than in his youth: his hair and gums
Are not as fair as once they were
If they were. You met him after
He could barely see and now he is
Almost blind, not seeing enough of the world
To see you whole. But you are doing
The looking, even in your chosen silence,

And I, like too many poets before me,
Have come up wanting in love's mirror
And have little business chasing figures
Of my own emptiness. Only your forgiveness
And patience leave a space for my foolishness
But I won't forget how partial these words.

64.

In your eyes along the streets can I see
The history of the place, the spirit
In the rain between Notre Dame

And the Sorbonne? I have no idea
Whether my grandfather came to this spot
When he lived here from 1888

To 1894. I never met him.
I'm vague about those of us who fled to England
And America, or the Normans who left

Long before. Is it luxury, homage
Or foolishness to imagine the past
In the eyes I meet? The rain has made us

Sodden. What would Héloïse and Abelard
Make of the students by the Hôtel Dieu?

65.

A Romanesque bridge joins one hill
To another for no apparent reason

And the mystery of this landscape
Is like the unknown territories

Of our bodies. A solitary tree
Blooms purple in the first green of spring.

The winters are not harsh here, not even
For lovers. I suppose there were purple

And green before the solstice: except
For the occasional snow, this is

A garden. But what do I know
About gardens but exile? Once sent

Eastward, is there any turning back?
We move blind among hedges, hills, power lines.

66.

Dusk falls over a land cut and crossed,
Road, rail, drive, path. Fields lie flooded

By the river. The philosophers are
All asleep. One kind of tree looks as though
It is full of eagle nests. Everywhere
Wires and wire fences filter the eye,
And the woods are framed by movement
And energy, the restlessness of this generation,
Its thirst for power. Historical
Geography is a love letter, which,
Some might add, has gone astray
Or bad. The moon will soon rise above the smoke.

Love does not dawn on us out of nature
But is written on the land, our skin.

.

67.

The country is not pastoral: it was
Fine for escaping the plague. Some would paint

Urban scenes on blinds in their carriages
Rather than look at the mess of some
Bucolic field. Now they are slaughtering

Sheep and cattle in this green and pleasant land
Where we once farmed, or, when we could,

Fled the wine trade for country life
London for East Anglia. What's remarkable
Is how the vast rural abattoir

Has now become a pyre, an army
Operation, for the love of country

What is to be done? By that stream in Cambridge
Were we deluded that nature could be loved?

68.

Nostalgia and utopia, past and future,
Absolve us of the present, but this impulse
To what was and will be is something

I at least cannot escape. It is
Another thing to falsify. We watch
Shadows on the wall, can try to fetch

Someone else's reality — a lover's,
An ancestor's, an unknown great-grandchild's
From an experience they hold. Time,

Distance, instinct, insight all help
The other to make some sense, but she
Has in all the tenses a world of her own

And I mine. This we is a fiction to live
In peace, the inscrutable angles of love.

69.

The nuclear power plants smoke over the land
In ways Petrarch, Newton and Marie Curie
Never knew: they light schools and houses
Even in the shadow of the Bomb. We, as slow

As we were, grew up under the threat, feared
We would have no children to tend
Or, rather, that we would never grow up.
The bomb shelter signs are still on the buildings

At Harvard, a yellow hazard, or they were there
Last time I looked. Here in eastern France
These stacks are a controversy
Out of sight for the children by the Seine.

What is it that takes us to death's threshold
As we glide on the rails with its power?

70.

The clouds lie over the land near Avignon
The train sweeps over the green: I recall
That time when I barely moved and where I lived
Had a mythology, was a kind of novel

Of facts and hearsay. That place in Montreal
Has emptied out, transformed far more
Than any medieval French village,
Even if the villagers moved more than we once thought.

Perhaps I am looking for the ghosts
Of childhood friends, although I have never
Met any of them in stations, roadstops
Or airports anywhere. The girls from school —

Sheila, Bente, Josée, Debbie — have fled
Into a materiality of their own.

71.

The cars on the rail line are stacked up
And through the electrification wires, I
Can barely see the sky. So much depends
On the sky. Dust hovers over the warehouses
Near Avignon station; spare rails lie
Down to the left side. Piles of earth sit
In mounds. The trackside Carrefour is backwards
Caravans on the left have a free view

Of the TGV. The bones of Petrarch
Share some of the traces of this soil.
We have parts of us that are millions
Of years old. Love and poetry are hard
To talk about in those terms. You smile
Although you, once here, are so far away now.

72.

Another poet scoffed when I said
I was writing love poems, although
What poems are not about desire
And exile, the memory of a mother's
Voice, the hope for a place free of pain

And death? Sometimes a poet will take us
Farther from the terrors of breath
And oblivion, leading us into the dread
That night was a relentless error
That gave birth to us as fear,

But then she will turn and imagine a space
As gentle and whole as God's grace, lifting
Heart and bone from pit and disappearance
As if her song of you and me were eternal.

73.

Why is it the poplar leaves turn in the sun
And catch it like water or fish, while I am
Too dull to do anything but drudge
And miss out on you. One day I will

Awaken, even though I have known
My fault all this time, and find you gone.
For a walk, or, never to return,
To another place not even science knows.

Why did we devise an economy
That makes us all slaves, some more, some less,
That drives people to sleep in the streets
Or others, more privileged, to bury themselves

In accounts, poems and profits, and neglect
The ones they love, who often dwell in fictions

74.

Made of systems? Love and justice have lost out
To work. Productivity is reproduction.

These joints are sore with work and ink.
Manuscripts are lost or eaten: buildings
Crumble; trusts are broken. Work chases
The death sentence we face. Belief

And psychosis attempt to make sense
Of the brute movement of time and nature.
It may be that we and our children fade
And are forgotten. But I will cast

My hope with you, my writing incidental
In your absence. That is my love song
As embarrassing as it is for all involved:
The smell of peach and daisies in our nostrils.

75.

The warehouses, spills, heaps, strews, broken waste
Crouch in the marshes across from Manhattan
The dead trees by the track I peer through

And squint as if I could see the natives
Watching Verrazzano from the shore
From marshes, beaches, woods as clean as trust

Under a blue sky. We are stalled in Secaucus
As far from Rouen, Avignon and Genoa
As Ulan Bator: the Indians are driven out

And the chain-link and leaning telephone poles
Tell little of my ancestor chased out of the Bronx —
And he died much later in Middletown —

Or of a beloved. In such dumping, scarring
Are songs false purity, virtual, askance?

76.

On an outcrop in Central Park, we talk
About leaves and geological time,
Consider the slant of sun on the green,
The lives of friends, their days by the Charles

Gone, while mothers push strollers amid spring
Sunbathers. The complexity of brick, stone, glass —
So many lives on this long slender finger
Between two rivers — drives us to science

And fiction, to putative lines between
Geology and poetry, the world and flesh
That the vendors ignore. We imagine space
Without books, the expanse of readers

Without a taste for paper. Nothing is binding
And we must part, you to your lab, I to my art.

77.

Girders and glass roofs extend at round
And sharp angles; some on the bottle glass
Broken in Newark Penn Station: some trains

Sit idle on Sunday. The World Trade Center
Peers through a waste of elevated highways,
Poles, wires, warehouses — airplanes lift

And land. Here it is hard to talk of love.
Chivalry gets lost in the graffiti.
Multi-storey parking garages stack up

Like stanzas. Smokestacks from refineries
Question the motives of poetry. To speak
Of your eyes in the twine of hydro lines

Is heroism or futility.
In this toxic trench will we live to love?

78.

Who would hear me above the surf, the remains
Of the day crumbling in a world read
Against the flight of emptiness? Love would call

A violin, old suffering on the cliffs
Tumbling into the sea. Odysseus didn't come
This far west or even farther by the pillars.

The rustle of an inscription for the dead
Leaves us a shell of socket and space
Dusted and borne back into an earth

Not even noticing. We are part
Of an unfolding, an unconscious force
That bears a beauty beyond poetry.

How does this music make our lives
A love more than a barren, something?

79.

The dead stars rise over the ridge, the garden
Tumultuous with texture, colour, the taste
Of pollen: nose, throat, eye all absorb

The lusting dust of spring. Something austere
Might move this blood and skin, resolve
Into a dew, a suspiration

Of a love that would endure past youth,
Beyond the gate that opens out on to
The sea. Can we be more than air

A breath not presumed or transposed
Into a record, a trace, a pledge
That would outlast the smallness of our hands?

I have a longing for you after all these years
And you most times nearby: these lips an orchard?

80.

My heart is even lonelier than my face
When you, away, and the children flee
The street for summer, and the space of night
Takes all day, leaves nowhere full, shakes the heart

Like a tree, and I, windfall inside and out,
Soundless like a task, fold in similitude
And cannot compare myself or anyone,
You, for instance, to a summer's day.

More lovely you, and quiet falls in my mind
Inarticulate as the flashing water
Flat to the horizon. The nameless dead
Of time reach for history, their love

Denied. These words are shadows, signatures,
Fools to oblivion: my love must be silent.

81.

Winter has its verges, not a green snow
Or a cut edge along the margin of a walk

And dancers squint out from their hoods
Kicking off mukluks, shedding parkas

As if this lake in the Shield were the great
Basin between Europe and Africa.

The taste of the chokecherries is too tart for death
But even a child sees mosquitoes die

And in that death his own, my own:
I remember: insects were hatching, buzzing,

Dying, slow-swift, in a movement beyond them.
Laws natural or divine so wanton.

Was it fig or apple or chokecherry —
Murderous ignorance, that moment always?

82.

Roses are more gorgeous than us: we are as birds
On the wind, taking in the pollen, feeling
The smooth pedals, a deeper red

Than blood. How do we love when death
Is in the air like a typology?
The grave-cradle of our breath and not

The urn of these woods — what can we do?
We can play and breathe hard as if there were
Too much air. We can stagger in a circus,

Tumble like acrobats, make more of us
To tumble more. We can embrace
And fashion as substitutes. We can make

Something more decent than cycle or machine
And hope there is some truth to this dream.

83.

Remember our mothers who bore us
And the children who will forget us
And the fruit that we were that will drop

Into the deep of the earth. The rapture
Of a sudden roaring world, the sea smashing
Shore outside my window, will always be

Us, hero, heroine, to our mother, father
And the turning away of time in a dream.
When we were children, we thought the old old

And now we know that was never so
That time speeds and eats flesh faster
Like a wasting disease, and we need to search,

Hold others to us, the world, to gather
As we are left more and more alone.

84.

The season of our wooing, a stillness now,
So frantic, bursting, pollinating then,
Makes nothing of twenty years. It is something

To us. Are stories enough of an argument
To say we were and are and will be?
Love is more than coffee spoons, even if

I gushed like a peach. This brain is getting
Too old for visions. Love poems are not
Self-help manuals. What do I know

That everyone else does not? I just happen
To have an ear and a pen at hand, a little
Like Bottom, to dream love is more than an ass

Nothing I can say is enough to celebrate
Fate, fortune, dumb luck, pleasure — meeting you.

85.

World, breath, disinherited us, even
Before we claimed to live, and slowly
We have tried to build back up what we have lost
In this ruined globe. Distracted

And unapprehending, we, lovers in the skeltered
Light, clutch at the sun, but it too is
A dying star. Roses die into
Eternity. We crave fixity, a love

To last past the trap of time. We are
An oversight, a draft in great sadness
Passed as fully formed. The accident
Of our touch might be a tenderness.

How do we leave the tombs of sleep behind
The door we make the window we shape?

86.

A certain happiness exists despite
The death sentence we all live under
And some will tell you it is not so

But I have seen it is. The gladness first
Baffled me, then came as a surprise
And I realized I was and would be blind

All my days. You might think something else
And as truth cannot be regulated
That's as it should be. Your golden hair

A nimbus on the beach by the farm
Blinded me in the best way, and your voice
Was as another world. And my feet were

On the ground. The span of our hands
Were something, of earth and ecstasy.

Ropes, planks, cups, lines, buckets, tiles, fieldstones
This is the inventory of our everyday lives
Touch them or break them and sometimes they will
Cut skin, nail, bone. Love is not angels alone

Or vows that rise up, inside and out,
Skies out on the sea beyond the cape
Or an internalized night sky. There might
Be something to that, but let's hope

Love is something discreet, with an inhereness
Not simply reduced to self-interest,
But not a self-sacrifice for that grace.
Even though I have read Ovid, my hands

Are not turning to leaves, yet. Why do I try
To understand you when I cannot myself?

88.

Pain like bread breaks and tears, and in France
The smell of dough is everywhere. I have
Given up weeping aloud. I was allowed

That at birth. I tread on stones like puns
Brittle, and where dogs go unrestricted
And make us dodge their assertions like bad

Metaphysics. I have loved you like the sun
On my skin, hot even in January
With its moulten pleasures, or the cool wind

That washes over us. I feel as if
I have betrayed our taciturn love
For the broken gods of words, and I'm not

Sure whether this iteration really becomes
The ripeness of our silence startled with gladness.

89.

Our whatever is an asymptote and not
It moves but never reaches, but does so
In ways that even we can observe.

And sometimes in our sleep we think we know
Better than we do, and, waking, we know
Even less. Catkins blow; dandelion seed

Sheds on the wind; fireflies flicker and flee
On the marsh. In love it is always spring
When it is not winter, and autumn

And summer expose that nonsense. Fools can
Love or try to, and we, fools in time,
Tumble, and, stumbling, we seek some axis.

Metaphors are like moonlight, and the sea is green
Even at night, the need of love embarrassing.

90.

It is not as if the sun and I

Have a unique relation, but the I

Of verse is stubborn and makes things up

To impress the world. Not that the world

Cares, and the sympathy of the trees

And the soul takes place in the mind

Or some vacancy the eye imagines.

And what of the heat of your breath, the smell

Of your hair, the sound of your words jousting

On the wind? The metaphor of love endures

In what it makes of itself, Troy long fallen,

A solar storm a trace. The window of the moon

Arises as though in a dream but language.

91.

The white cliffs above Cassis
Conceal the ache of exile after months here
The winter-spring of the changing light, voices
Of my children vanished by the coast: gone

Like traces, love on the run, nature turning
The sun-wind whispering through olive leaves
And friends, their laughter, fleeting like mythology.
The train hissing around the bend as only French trains

Can. The also-rans and run-ons of breath
And texture bend around corners. These moments
Break out of my lungs and fingers: the song
Of words will not leave me alone. The haze

Over the green land wraps itself out of focus
But in spots the sun is as clear as love.

92.

The shadows of the evening still across
Your eyes, the recalcitrance of age takes up
These bones as if time could lie, and the sky

You longed for waits for the blind night
And the youth we lose is a gambler's wheel
That exacts the guilt of cliché. Our night

Minds bombard us with types: the babble
Of radio, video, portable phone, the trample
Of internet, the numb hum of TV

All make light of body and soul. Bury my heart
In discourse, like radio waves for aliens
And lay us out in a script. The ineffable

Unthing that is us, and of us, is up against
The darkness nature, and we, make for us.

93.

For him, there is only one poet: his wife.
All the others lack something, unless
Perhaps they are dead. Love is like that

Sometimes. The moon over the Caspian
Is not like that over Rome, or was it
The Black Sea? It's the ground like a premise

That is a lunatic conclusion
Already. The wind carries the rain
Like memory. In her words his youth lies

And in her eyes her words almost.
The asymptote of desire defies
An exactness that desire wants. So for us

The rain freezes on the heath and we,
Homeless, are naked before the stars.

94.

Something rebarbative lives in this life
The mirror gets harder with each year
And all the flaws on its surface and mine
Become more apparent in the illusion

Of time. I never thought I would be young
For ever but did, not knowing how bones
Age and faces thicken, like hands, and necks
Or how the weariness of the brain sets in

And the mouth tastes like cigarettes in beer
Floating, when people used to smoke and use
Bottles as ashtrays. But age
Is not a simile: it just is, and the grave

Awaits and aches lost love. And the earth,
Error, nags at the waste I have become.

95.

These eyes, joints, gums ache with an age
That one day wakes up, unencumbered,
The wind not even noticing, the moon
Not even an emblem of change: the tides

Wash up and time won't even try
To have hands. Why does the moment
Flee backwards, and then it is too late
Like love? One day youth has fled

And the winter hides its offensive
Below the summer ground. And your eyes
Look astonished that after so few years
I am bent, torn, reeling, devious

Sometimes before the foe. But this isn't
A battle: there can be no triumph. But love.

96.

You watch the dying light after the star
Is dead, something that is but is not,
And I see you by the window by the sea

And all seems like a force, palpable
But not tangible, verbs turned adjectives
The hair of a dead grandmother in a case

Refracting light our eyes cannot see.
Love is a cosmography, a strange
Mathematics of desire and memory.

Your mind reflects on itself, a beauty
Poets can only hope for, the sun on your sleeve.

97.

There's something about a train that is like
A sonnet: how promising is that?
The movement of lines, the rhythm, sound, friction

Whatever the comparison, trains make
Poems. Songs can rail against love,
The scarring like the marshalling yards

On land that once was pasture. Country thoughts
Are not always pastoral. Love is now
Industrial strength: white noise and image-thrust

Lust after whatever sublimation is left
But the whisper of your hand is deft.

98.

On the brink of simile I faced
The failure of words to describe the world
Ineffable as the horizon beyond the sea
The wash, where the fens were drained,

Rivers silted and ports waned, inconstant
As time and love. Blame it on time: something,
Someone has to give. The dark church of our heart
Stains the glass of the incoming light,

Glows over the graveyard, full of old loves
And broken hopes. The yew by the wall leans
Into the wind, your smile, the children
Play games down the path. The edge of time

Sharpens our bones, betrayal,
Ambivalence: yet your eye is firm.

99.

Your heart is knapped flint, or is it mine?
I had not realized you were a kittiwake
Building a deep nest in my heart. You nearly,
Or more nearly I, ruined what I had

But made we nearly made me, towards
The end of youth, not knowing how brittle
The mind is, how close to soul, heart, bone
It had come. There were sole, plaice, brill, cod, even

Dogfish at the stalls, once slithering on the boats
After the haul. My words are herring, red
And otherwise, finding hook, line, net
Sunk. The heat of blood, the fade of recollection

Vanish past the pier. A love that is not the love:
The mind gulled on the beach at dusk.

100.

Love is a Stonehenge, virtual to some,
Palpable to others, a circle,
A temple, a long haul. Perhaps it is

The orientation of the light, the stone brought
All that way to make something splendid,
In common. Explanations are rains

That pelt, drench, mist and fall from
The monument. The metaphysics of love
Falls back on the physical world: bodies

Abide beneath the sun. What sacrifices
Are made for the unspoken, unseen?
Your face is round before the moon. Time hides

What we want most: we dig and say to regain
The garden, bring gods into our bones.

101.

The hills are burial mounds: the oaks drape
Drives by the houses — the invention

Of private lives dwells beyond the windows
And some tenderness arises amid

The diurnal wars. Over the hedges,
Where lavender reaches, there is life

Not entirely prone to venality
And lust. The rain has started, but it's not

The end of the world. The sky has turned
To shale, and the ghost of a king rails

On the heath. He is angry at love,
Forgets his absent wife, blames his daughters,

Vanishes into myth. The taut train rushes
Into the valley, the land some consolation.

102.

The Georgian calms the world about, hills slant
Asky, the round and crescent relieve
The eye, and love has known its time here

From Romans to the landed, the Avon
Downstream from a boy who could shape
A mean sonnet, the stench of gloves still

In his pores. These love poems wind like
This river, its dark glass now reflecting
Cloud and tree on the train window, and distance

Is left like a tempo, and similes
Squirm like adolescents in love, and seek
Your touch with you away. Tongues have souls

And this is beyond proof, love is a silence
Beyond strife, held, the elm on the hill your thumb.

103.

The speculation of music has
An invisible sound, the ear-mind reading
Without play, the dream of a universal
Language moving like wind in chimes

On a porch at the cottage by the lake
The glaciers left where birds sang and muskrat
Rustled in the rushes before Pythagoras
Made harmony a theory. Love appeals

To the senses, agape its own music
Of the spheres. When I hear you in the kitchen
Singing to yourself, alone with the sun
On the table, or feel children playing

Through the floorboards, I recall how small hands
Can express the sound of the gods in love.

104.

We rose from dust on a day not of our
Choosing, the wind on our mothers' brows
Cut lines, the glaciers were receding

Imperceptibly, and we shrieked
Not knowing who we were. There was nothing
Socratic about the doctors; the nurses

Dreamt of love, perhaps, but were too practical
And their sensible shoes imposed stereotype
And the wolves in the canyons were long silent.

The trees had been cut, although no one
Spoke of hell, not even in hushed tones.
Lover and beloved could not talk then

And our lungs, whichever we were, thrilled more
For air than for metaphysical hyperbole.

105.

The wind was slapping the water, and the surf
Mounted like whale-spout, the weather

Was out for blood. I thought of Nantucket
And the Vineyard, how those ancestors

Could turn for love when the ships and docks
Were seeped with blood. The Quakers there shook

Before the law. I may be conflating time,
But that is how the wind shook me, taking

Mind-hand into a net of metaphor.
But the wind is the wind, and water water

And slapping is what Hermes left at the door
Even suggesting that your breath is what makes

Love a wind and words, breathed, lovely.
No wonder lovers want to be left alone.

106.

What of the furtive thief of love stealing
Nothing expected when youth had time enough
And coyness went out with roaring headlines
And electronic images too obscene for the gods?

The reeds from your fingers reassure me
That you have not been eaten online
Or on some couch by some film or slime
Where people are too good for other people,

But can that rest, some caesura, come
In the thunderous rage and chat of our time?
The struggle for love, a secret garden
Amid battle, has raged so long. Hands have

Stacked skulls at Golgotha, Moscow and Treblinka
Stolen tears beading on broken fingernails.

107.

You don't have to be Richard the Third
To have night terrors: the wound of guilt,
Hurt, death calls on all of us, even those

Who seem to believe the advertising.
What shadows cut our minds at night
And shake our days with the sweet heat

Of hidden ice? Hell is here, not just
For monsters and fallen angels. It haunts
The light on the fields, the trenches of then

And now. The tyrants there and within threaten
The good we were born to. Slogans
Are hidden tales, various as our desires.

Perhaps there's a history of love without Sade
And Richard's rape of Anne in the Abbey.

108.

How to keep the deep fluster and rush
Of blood and flesh that make us animal
From destroying the filament, firmament
We would become? Ancient images

But they catch some of the dilemma,
The molecule between lust and love,
Orgazma extravaganza and ecstasy,
The mixed apprehension of sense and idea.

That may be too abstract as we touch
The tablecloth, the sun on your face flush
And the blush of summer upon us, the smell
Of lilies too soon to fester. Must we be

Volcanoes, the unpredictable eruption,
And can the lava cool and flowers bloom there?

109.

The barges slip along the Seine, the wind has died
By Notre Dame: the heat of August burns the stone
Even as the night has come. The winter of our hearts

Is gone, and your absence here is the only
Way this city lacks. The moon is snow
Over the Sorbonne, the voice of Héloïse

Fleeing down the few crooked streets Haussmann left.
The avenues are gorgeous, but love is seldom
Linear. It would be folly to lose

Paris or you to metaphor. At Christmas
We will come here and watch the shadows
Between the ruined trees and remember.

Love is in the place and flees the types
Words might make: the river is our breath.

Acknowledgements

As I have given detailed thanks in earlier books, I will keep these acknowledgements brief. There are many people over many years and in many places to whom I owe gratitude. To those who have encouraged my poetry — poets, friends, editors, teachers, translators, and readers — and to the poets who went before, my thanks.

At Athabasca University Press, my thanks to Manijeh Mannani, series editor, and to Walter Hildebrandt, director, Pamela MacFarland Holway, senior editor, and Natalie Olsen, designer. My thanks also to the two anonymous readers.

Musing was written in Europe and North America and was completed in France in the summer of 2001. I wish to thank colleagues at Princeton University, the University of Cambridge, the University of Alberta, and the Camargo Foundation, in Cassis (my thanks also to the director and to the foundation itself). To Deborah Elder, my gratitude for the use of her beautiful print for the cover. To my translators, Maria Athanasopoulou (Greek), Wladimir Krysinski (Polish), Nicole Mallet (French), Jüri Talvet (Estonian), and Nadezda Vashkevich (Russian), my thanks.

To Gordon Teskey, my gratitude for his generous introduction.

To friends and family, many thanks once more — George Edward Hart, my father; Charles, Gwendolyn, Deborah, Alan, and Jennifer, my brothers and sisters; Mary Marshall, and our children, Julia and James.

I dedicate this book most particularly to George and Mary.

Jonathan Locke Hart
Summer 2010

Index of First Lines

JONATHAN LOCKE HART has published poetry for over twenty-five years in literary journals such as *Cimarron Review*, *Grain*, *Harvard Review*, *Mattoid*, *Quarry*, and *The Antigonish Review*. Translations of his poems have been published in Estonian, French, Greek, and other languages. He has given readings in Australia, Canada, Estonia, France, Germany, Slovenia, the United Kingdom, the United States, and elsewhere. His recent volumes of poetry are *Breath and Dust* (2000), *Dream China* (2002), *Dream Salvage* (2003), and *Dreamwork* (2010). Professor Hart began teaching at the University of Alberta in 1984 and has also held visiting appointments at Cambridge, Harvard, Princeton, Sorbonne Nouvelle, Toronto, and Zaragosa.

ℂ This book was typeset in Bembo, a Monotype design based on a roman typeface cut by Francesco Griffo in Italy in 1495.